IDEA/WISE Fireplaces

Inspiration & Information for the Do-It-Yourselfer

Jerri Farris

Creative Publishing international

CHANHASSEN, MINNESOTA
www.creativepub.com

D1444423

Creative Publishing
international

Copyright © 2006
Creative Publishing international, Inc.
18705 Lake Drive East
Chanhassen, Minnesota 55317
1-800-328-3895
www.creativepub.com

Printed in Singapore

10 9 8 7 6 5 4 3 2 1

President/CEO: Ken Fund

Publisher: Bryan Trandem

Author: Jerri Farris
Senior Art Director: Dave Schelitzche
Photo Editor: Julie Caruso
Technical Illustrator: Earl Slack
Assistant Managing Editor: Tracy Stanley
Production Manager: Linda Halls
Proofreader: Barb Jacobs

IdeaWise: Fireplaces

Library of Congress Cataloging-in-Publication Data

Farris, Jerri.
  Fireplaces : inspiration & information for the do-it-yourselfer / Jerri Farris.
      p. cm. -- (Ideawise)
  Includes bibliographical references.
  Summary: "Provides readers with inspiration for using
decorative fire features in home and yard decor. Features the
very latest in flame technology, firebox construction, and
building materials"--Provided by publisher.
    ISBN-13: 978-1-58923-281-5 (soft cover)
    ISBN-10: 1-58923-281-X (soft cover)
1. Fireplaces--Design and construction--Amateurs' manuals.
2. Do-it-yourself work. I. Title. II. Series.
  TH7425.F37 2006
  697'.1--dc22
                                        2006011060

Table of Contents

Introduction

For centuries fireplaces have provided not only the hearth, but the very heart of millions of homes. Their warmth and beauty long ago wedged themselves into our collective consciousness in such a way that many of us don't truly feel we're home until the fire is lit. The National Association of Home Builders reports that fireplaces rank among the top three features desired by buyers of new homes, but even without a survey, almost anyone could tell you that people genuinely love fireplaces and are instinctively drawn to gather around them.

Small wonder that so many people want to include a fireplace in their home. Industry experts estimate that a fireplace adds as much as $12,000 to the value of a house. Of course, that number varies by home and by region as well as by the fireplace itself, but there's no question that a fireplace adds real value in terms of dollars and in terms of the daily enjoyment of your home.

The history of fire—and of fireplaces—is the history of humankind itself. No one knows the origins of fire, although every culture provides myths and legends to explain its presence in our lives. Many of these stories involve stealing fire from the gods, as though only divinity could supply something so magical and mystical.

No matter its provenance, fire has been around so long that it's represented in even the earliest human art and traces of its use are found in the remains of even the earliest civilizations. At first, of course, these were open fires, found outside dwellings and eventually located at their center. Laws to regulate the use of fire were recorded by the 11th century. In fact, the word curfew, (meaning time for everyone to be home behind closed doors) is derived from the term for a metal device designed to cover the fire at night.

Although no one knows exactly when or where the first true fireplace was built, chimneys as we know them had become common by the middle of the 14th century, and the years since have been marked by improvements in the design and functionality of fireplaces.

And that brings us neatly to today, when concerns about the availability and environmental impact of various energy sources have brought fireplaces and stoves to the forefront of the war on rising heating costs.

If you have followed the news at all, by now you know that uncovered wood-burning fireplaces drain heat from a home rather than add to it. What you may not know is that if you have a wood-burning fireplace in need of renovation, you're in good company: the average wood-burning fireplace is 23 years old and could use a little sprucing up in the technological sense as well as the design sense. The average gas fireplace is less than five years old, but there are older versions out there that could use help, too.

Most new homes of today are being built with at least one fireplace, and the choice is not one you want to leave to the contractor. Only you know how and why and when your family will use the fireplace and what you would most enjoy.

So, whether you're renovating a fireplace, adding one during a remodeling project, or including one (or more) in a new home, you've come to the right place. The pages of IdeaWise Fireplaces are filled with images, ideas, and information that will help you select and design a fireplace that fits within your budget, suits your lifestyle, and delights your senses.

How to use this book

The pages of *IdeaWise Fireplaces* are packed with images of fireplaces and heating stoves used in real-life room settings, both as practical sources of heat and as decorative features contributing to the style and atmosphere of homes.

Study these examples carefully as you consider how to decorate with fire in your own home. Carefully study the examples found on the following pages. They'll give you ideas for how to best integrate a fire feature into your home, and also give you information on state-of-the-art technologies that may change how you think about fireplaces.

IdeasWise Fireplaces includes seven chapters: Options, Living Rooms, Family Rooms & Great Rooms, Bedrooms, Kitchens & Dining Areas, Outdoor Rooms, and Decorating Fireplaces. Options will give you an overview of fireplace choices and technologies, while the other chapters will show you how to integrate various fire features into the different spaces in your home. And keep an eye open for the various helpful tip boxes and sidebars—they offer indispensible insider tips and techniques.

*Dolla*rWise

Turning down the flames on a gas fireplace makes sense: smaller flames consume less gas. On the control panel of your gas fireplace, you should find a knob with markings ranging from HIGH to LOW. Dial down the flames and you'll dial down the cost of running the fireplace, too.

CHAPTER 1

Options

Once you've decided that you want to include, add, or renovate a fireplace, the real fun begins. You're faced with a myriad of options regarding style and function, each with long lists of potential advantages and disadvantages to consider.

There is no one right choice, and that means the only way to proceed is to evaluate your needs and determine which option meets most of them. Many people—most, in fact—consider a fireplace to be largely a design feature, but there is so much more than style involved in this decision. To make an informed choice, you'll need to consider fuel cost, efficiency, cleanliness, environmental impact, and ease of use.

This chapter will prepare you to ask the right questions and evaluate the answers you receive from the retailers, contractors, designers, and installers with whom you work on this project.

Fireplaces

Statistics indicate that if your home is more than five years old and has a working fireplace, that fireplace probably burns wood. On the other hand, if your home is less than five years old, there's a very good chance that your fireplace burns gas. If you're adding a fireplace, studies tell us that there's a better than ever chance you're going to choose a gas appliance. This shift in popularity is credited to the convenience, cost, and environmental advantages of gas fireplaces. And, while these are the statistical probabilities, they say little about what is best for your home and family.

Most homeowners burn fireplaces for reasons that are more emotional than practical. In other words, they burn them not to heat their homes but to warm their hearts and psyches. Still, a fireplace represents a substantial investment and it's important to choose an efficient, easy to use fireplace that complements the style of your home and the style of your life.

At one time, most fireplaces were custom-built structures created by skilled masons. They required substantial foundations and careful, time-consuming construction. As labor costs skyrocketed and the supply of skilled masons dwindled, pre-fabricated fireplace inserts emerged in the market. These units are lighter, which means they require less structural support, and self-contained, which means they require less labor-intensive installation. Although it is still possible to have a masonry fireplace built, it can be a very expensive proposition.

Conventional fireplaces take more heat out of a room than they add, but most fireplace inserts produce a net heat gain. To update a masonry fireplace, you can have an EPA certified insert installed inside a masonry firebox or in an approved metal firebox.

Many cities have "no burn" days and ordinances that prohibit the building of any wood-burning fireplaces in new construction. EPA-approved inserts produce 90 percent fewer emissions than traditional fireplaces and are approved for use even on high pollution days in many communities.

Traditional wood-burning fireplaces can also be converted to gas fireplaces by adding a vented or vent-free log set or a gas insert. For any gas option, you have to run a gas line. Gas lines should be run only by a licensed plumber or HVAC technician.

A gas insert is a completely contained (closed) unit, basically a box with a gas burner inside and a glass front. Gas fireplace inserts usually are 12 to 16 inches deep and four feet high and anywhere from three to five feet wide. Inserts burn clean, they're cost effective, and they require little maintenance. It's true that they don't produce the crackling sounds so many people love, but neither do they produce ashes or particulate pollution. They're also incredibly easy to operate—they can be controlled by remotes, wall switches, or thermostats.

Conventional fireplaces also can be made more efficient by adding electric, coal-, or pellet-burning inserts.

When adding a fireplace, all options are in play. If your budget allows, you can have installed a traditional masonry fireplace. If an investment of that size doesn't make sense to you, choose one of a variety of inserts: wood burning, gas, electric, pellet burning, or coal.

Stoves

Unlike fireplaces, heating stoves produce a net gain in heat, and many savvy homeowners know it. According to industry sources, 66 percent of stove owners use their stoves specifically to save on heating costs. And use them they do: 83 percent of stove owners fire them up 12 to 24 times a year compared to 58 percent of fireplace owners.

Wood- and coal-burning stoves have been around for generations. More recently, they've been joined by gas, electric, pellet- and corn-burning stoves. The heat output of wood- and coal-burning stoves is controlled by the amount of fuel you add, but with gas, electric, pellet- and corn-burning stoves output is controlled by an electronic thermostat. This means they require less supervision and are less work than wood- or coal-burning stoves. Gas and electric stoves require virtually no effort, and although pellet and corn stoves must be fed, they can hold several days worth of fuel at one time. "Stoker" coal stoves have self-feeding mechanisms that reduce the work of maintaining their fire, too.

(The following information is accurate for both stoves and fireplace inserts.)

 Wood Most are easy to install, and many are quite attractive. They are also messy, and keeping them burning requires a fair amount of work—bringing in wood, filling stove, cleaning up dust and bark, and removing ashes.

Gas Easy to use and maintain; most are easy to install. Most can accommodate either natural gas or propane with slight modifications.

 *Electric* Require very little installation other than wiring and require little maintenance. Electric stoves vary in their realism, but most produce reliable, economical heat with almost no effort on the part of the homeowner. Some people also appreciate the fact that the heat and light of most electric fires are operated independently, which means you can "turn on the fire" even when it's too warm for a real fire.

 *Pellets* Burn cleanly and are exempt from most restrictive ordinances. Adding an imitation log set makes the fire look better. If power outages are a factor in your area, it's a good idea to have a backup power source so the stove's augur can work when the power is out. In most communities, freestanding pellet stoves supported by a pedestal or legs have to be installed over non-combustible flooring. Pellet stoves require a fair amount of maintenance: You have to empty the ash traps and clean the exhaust passages behind the fire chamber, clean and lubricate the fans and motors, clean the hopper and fuel feed system, as well as the heat exchanger system and exhaust pipes, and reseal the venting system when necessary.

Corn

Corn stoves are all the rage these days, and many stores are selling them as fast as they can be unloaded. The advantages are pretty obvious: the stoves themselves are reasonably priced and so is the fuel. Plus, corn is a readily renewable resource that produces little environmental impact. These stoves have augur systems that transfer the fuel from the hopper to the firepot. Check the design of the stove to make sure the firepot and heat exchange system are easy to clean. Corn can be burned in many stoves manufactured to burn pellets, but check with manufacturer first. Also make sure the right type of corn is available in your area—it may be harder to come by in urban areas.

 Coal

Coal is most efficient when burned in freestanding stoves. Some stoves are dual-fuel, capable of burning wood or coal. These stoves should be installed only by someone with experience. Although coal stoves last 10 years or more, it's common to replace coal grates and liners over the years. With most coal stoves, you have to shake the coals once a day when there is a hot fire, and remove the ashes before they accumulate above the top of the ash pan. With a stoker stove, you only need to add coal to the hopper every two or three days, but you still have to empty the ash pan every day or two. Coal stoves don't produce creosote or tar, but they do produce fine ash. This ash is quite corrosive when combined with heat and humidity, so the stove, smoke pipe, and chimney have to be cleaned at the end of each burning season. You need barriers to keep small children and family pets away from the hot surfaces of a coal stove. Finally, coal may not be readily available in all areas: Check before investing in a coal stove.

Fuel

Which fuel is least expensive depends on where you live and what's readily available to you. According to a Penn State University professor in December of 2005, here are the costs to generate a million BTUs with various fuels

Propane	$33.80
Natural Gas	$16.47
Pellets	$11.50
Corn	$ 8.75

Although the Penn State study didn't include coal, other studies indicate that it costs about $8.00 to generate a million BTUs with coal.

Fuel prices vary widely from one season to another, so it's best to compare the most current prices available. To find a computerized calculator search "Fuel Cost Comparison Calculator" on the internet and follow the instructions found there.

Wood

Firewood usually is sold by a measurement called a "cord" or fraction of a cord. A standard cord is 8 ft. long by 4 ft. wide by 4 ft. high, 128 cubic feet when stacked in a line or row.

Burn only wood with a moisture content of less than 20 percent. Hardwood (oak, madrone, hickory, and ash) burns cleaner than softwood (fir, pine, and cedar). It's fine to buy freshly cut or "green" wood, as long as you know that's what you're getting and you have 8 to 12 months for it to dry properly before you burn it.

Logs more than 6 inches in diameter should be split into smaller pieces, and sized to fit into your fireplace or stove.

In most states, sellers are required to provide an invoice that shows the seller's name, address, phone number, price per cord, and the type of wood purchased.

To store firewood, buy or build a rack that keeps the logs at least 10 inches off the ground. (You can create a simple rack by supporting two 2 × 4s between concrete blocks.)

Stack the firewood as far from the house as practical—you don't want the insects and other pests that can lurk in logs to take up residence in your house. Since bark repels water, stack the logs with the bark toward the top. When you buy new logs, rotate the ones at the bottom of the stack to the top—don't store logs at the bottom of the stack for more than a year. Cover the wood with a plastic tarp during severe weather.

How to Start a Wood Fire

- Use dry, split kindling and newspaper to set the fire.
- Open the damper.
- Twist a separate piece of newspaper into a torch and light it at one end. Hold the burning torch up to the damper to warm the flue.
- When the draft is established, light the kindling.
- After the kindling is burning, add larger pieces of wood. Be careful not to smother the fire with pieces that are too large.

Remember:

- Don't overload the firebox.
- Don't burn garbage or waste, especially gift wrappings or evergreen boughs.
- Never burn treated wood containing pesticides.

Gas

Natural gas and propane are clean burning, efficient, and easy to acquire. Although natural gas prices have risen sharply of late, many people are willing to pay the price for the convenience and simplicity of gas fireplaces and stoves.

Not all homes are supplied with natural gas, but most fireplaces and stoves work equally well with propane, which you can buy in bulk and store in a tank in the yard. Running gas lines is a job for a professional.

 *Electricity*

Available in all but the most remote locations, electricity is clean, easy to use, and virtually maintenance free. If you like the appearance of an electric fire device, the only remaining drawback is that it can't be used as an auxiliary heat source when the power goes out.

 *Pellets*

Pellets are made from sawdust and ground wood chips—waste materials from wood used to make furniture, lumber, and other products. After the base material is compressed, resins and binders that occur naturally in the sawdust hold the pellets together so most contain no additives. Pellets come in 40-lb. bags and are sold by the bag or by the ton (usually 50 bags on a shipping pallet). The cost of pellets averages between $150 and $200 per ton, but that varies by region, availability, and season. A ton of pellets can be stacked in an area as small as four feet wide, long, and high—about half as much space as you need for a cord of wood. Pellets can be stored in a dry garage, basement, or utility room.

Corn

Dried, shelled corn with a moisture content between 14 and 15% can be used for fuel. The corn, which can be purchased in bags or bulk containers, needs to be stored in a clean, dry place not open to rodents, birds, or squirrels. If the corn is in bags, they should be stacked on a pallet rather than on the floor. If it's in a bulk container, the container shouldn't be sealed—air needs to circulate around and through the corn.

Shelled corn is generally sold by the bushel or by weight. One bushel of shelled corn with a moisture content of about 15% weighs 56 pounds.

 Coal

Anthracite coal, the hardest type of coal, has a very high heat value and is best for heating. Anthracite produces virtually no smoke, particulates, or creosote as it burns so there is no threat of chimney fires. Coal suppliers say that coal is abundant and using it is good for the economy. One ton of anthracite coal is equal to 180 gallons of fuel oil, 7325 kilowatts of electricity, 298 gallons of propane, or 1.47 tons of wood pellets.

How to Clean Glass Doors

Use a special fireplace glass door cleaner. Check manufacturers recommendations, and follow them. It's best to remove the glass if you can, but they can be cleaned in place if necessary. When cleaning the doors, check the gaskets and seals. Lubricate the glass clips.

Gas stoves doors don't usually get very dirty unless there is a combustion problem. If yours seem excessively dirty, have the fireplace checked right away.

Fireplace Safety

When it comes to fireplaces, cleanliness is next to... safety. Inside and out, fireplaces need to be clean and in good working order. Here are some essential safety tips:

- Have your fireplace inspected and cleaned at least once a year by a certified chimney sweep.
- Before the first fire of the season, shine a flashlight up the flue to check for birds' nests or other obstructions.
- Trim overhanging branches or large trees near your chimney.
- Always use a fireplace screen. Leave glass doors open (if you have them), but draw the mesh screen over the opening.
- Never leave a fire unattended. Be sure the fire is out before you leave the house or go to bed.
- Use only the fuel for which the fireplace was intended.
- Never use a lighter fluid or any other accelerant to start or enlarge a fire.
- When building a wood fire, put the logs on a grate positioned toward the rear of the fireplace.
- Read and follow label instructions when using manufactured logs.
- Keep a fire extinguisher near each fireplace. Test the extinguisher annually and teach all family members how to use it.
- Install smoke detectors throughout the house. Test each detector every three months or so and replace the batteries annually.
- Place a carbon monoxide detector in each room with a fireplace and make sure they are working at all times.
- Keep the area around the fireplace clean and clear.
- Make sure the ashes are completely cold before removing them. Even if you're sure they're cold, always carry ashes out of the house in a metal containter.

CHAPTER 2

Living Rooms

I t's such a cozy image: a blazing fire, a good book, and a comfortable chair. For most people, images like that come to life in what's often called a "living room." It's an inexact term, to be sure, for what is a living room to one person may be a family room or hearth room or den to another. For the purposes of this book, when we use that term, we're describing rooms that are used mainly for entertaining, conversing, reading, listening to music, and so on.

Living rooms often are the most formal room in a house, and it's that very formality that leads the way when it comes to decisions about the fireplace found therein. Wood-burning fireplaces are delightful but the attendant mess can be exasperating in formal rooms. Gas fireplaces are easy and painless to use but their "instant" nature doesn't suit every room. Few stoves of any sort are at home in truly formal rooms but there are exceptions, depending on both the room and the stove.

In the formality of a living room, a fireplace serves an architectural function, and it's important that its shape, style, and the materials it includes are consistent with the room's design.

It all adds up to this: think carefully about your living room—how it's used, who uses it, and when—as you look through this chapter for ideas and inspiration that can be translated to your own home.

Picture-frame molding brings the perceived height of the room down a bit, which helps the fireplace anchor the space.

The columns on either side of the mantel are modeled after the columns in the room.

A formal living room dictates a rather formal fireplace, such as this one. The marble surround and finely wrought wood mantel set the tone for the fireplace and the room beyond.

A firescreen and raised hearth shield the fine rug from sparks and embers.

The overmantel flares out in an inverted reflection of the shaped ceiling.

Uplights mimic the upward sweep of the flames.

Small, easy-to-move chairs can be drawn nearer the fire on cold nights or pulled over to the conversation areas when desired.

A subtle black front blends into the surroundings rather than calling attention to itself.

The fireplace ledge serves as a sort of mantel, where antique Japanese teapots reside peacefully. A Japanese-style lantern glows on the hearth, providing warm light when the fire is not lit.

A muted pattern in the wallpaper and live plants soften the angular lines of the room.

The brick fireplace in this remodeled Craftsman home exudes a Zen-like serenity, as does the room.

A Japanese-style lantern glows on the hearth, providing warm light when the fire is not lit.

Graceful shades float on delicate stems, much like the lovely orchids on the coffee table.

Bookshelves embrace an enormous stone fireplace, filling the room with light and warmth in many ways. Gas fireplaces, such as this one, can be equipped with a rheostat to turn the blower up or down. This feature decreases the time it takes to warm the room, but it also allows you to enjoy the fire when temperatures are more moderate.

An art deco fireplace and mantel bridges the gap between this modern furniture, antique accents, and a striking African sculpture.

Create a fireplace that fits the room.

Family portraits displayed above the mantel seem to be the raison d'etre for the room itself. The height of the mantel, the colors of the rug and furnishings, the navy-blue walls—all are keyed off of some aspect of the lovely artwork. It may be a bit unconventional, but if you have treasures that you know will be displayed above the fireplace, design the fireplace to accommodate them.

An ornate mantel and surround complement the cove molding around the room and the cornice-board trim over the leaded glass windows in this living room. By integrating the most striking elements in the room, the homeowners tied them together into a magnificent vignette rather than allowing them to compete with one another for attention.

A soaring white stucco fireplace sandwiched between a mellow wood floor and lofty beamed ceiling dominates this living room. The hearth includes bench seating as well as storage niches, and the multi-level ledges double as a mantel and display space.

The cream sofas and walls seem to create a funnel through which the eye is drawn to this fireplace. The use and placement of color, accents, and lighting direct attention to the center of the room.

Surrounded by stucco walls and a tile hearth,

a pellet stove radiates warmth into this southwestern-style living room. If you choose a pellet stove for a living room, look for one with a quiet auger system so the family moments aren't disturbed by the sound of the stove feeding itself. An easy-to-clean firebox is especially important in a living room, where you won't want to spread ashes on valuable rugs and furnishings.

Cement masquerades as marble surrounding this coal-burning fireplace. Today's cement can be shaped, colored, and polished in surprising—and surprisingly sophisticated—ways. Carefully consider the weight of the structure and the support it will require before deciding on cement, but don't be afraid to use it liberally if conditions allow.

Before choosing a coal-burning fireplace or stove, check local suppliers for availability and prices.

Adding a fire screen lets you keep the doors open so you can hear and see the fire.

Wood can be loaded from the front or the side of the stove.

The handles are made to be safe to touch.

When placing a stove in front of a fireplace, look for legs that position the stove where you want it. Special "hearth legs" often are available.

A petite, enamel wood-burning stove sits in front of a non-working fireplace in this cheerful room. A stove like this can be used in many places you wouldn't normally find fireplaces—even in mobile homes.

An electric insert was fit into an existing masonry fireplace, replacing a non-functioning fireplace with an attractive, efficient unit. The insert front creates a realistic appearance and the attractive flames produce genuine warmth.

The living room as well as the gathering room beyond are warmed by this see-through fireplace. Each side of a see-through insert can be finished to complement the room it faces, creating a distinct look for each room.

Words to the Wise

Ash pit: : an area where ashes can be collected for disposal (not found in gas and electric fireplaces)

Chimney: : the vertical structure that houses the fireplace flue

Damper: : a mechanical flap or door between the smoke chamber and the firebox. The damper is used to control the draft. It must be open when a fire is burning and closed after the fire is out. (If the damper is left open, warm air from the room escapes up the flue and out of the house.)

Firebox: : the masonry center of the fireplace. The firebox contains the actual fire.

Firebrick: : refractory brick capable of withstanding extreme temperatures.

Flue: : a vertical channel inside the chimney. The flue runs from the smoke chamber to the top of the chimney. Its job is to create a draft and discharge the smoke.

Foundation: : a reinforced concrete structure that supports the weight of the fireplace

Inner Hearth: : firebox floor, made of firebrick

Lintel: : a piece of angle iron that spans the fireplace opening. The lintel supports the weight of the decorative face of the fireplace.

Mantel: : a shelf mounted above the fireplace. Usually made of wood, masonry, or stone.

Outer Hearth: : (also known as a hearth extension) an extension of the firebox, made of brick, stone, or another non-combustible material.

Overmantel: : the facing between the mantel and the ceiling. Not found on every fireplace.

Smoke Chamber: : An angled section between the firebox and the flue. The smoke chamber allows smoke and combustion gases to rise to the flue. It is angled to rebuff downdrafts.

Smoke Shelf: : a flat shelf that protects the firebox by catching falling soot.

Spark arrestor: : a metal-mesh guard between the top of the chimney flue and the chimney cap. Intended to keep sparks inside the chimney and rain and animals out of it.

Surround: : the facing around the top and sides of the fireplace opening. Must be made from a non-combustible material, such as tile, brick, or stone.

Throat: : A narrow opening between the firebox and the smoke chamber.

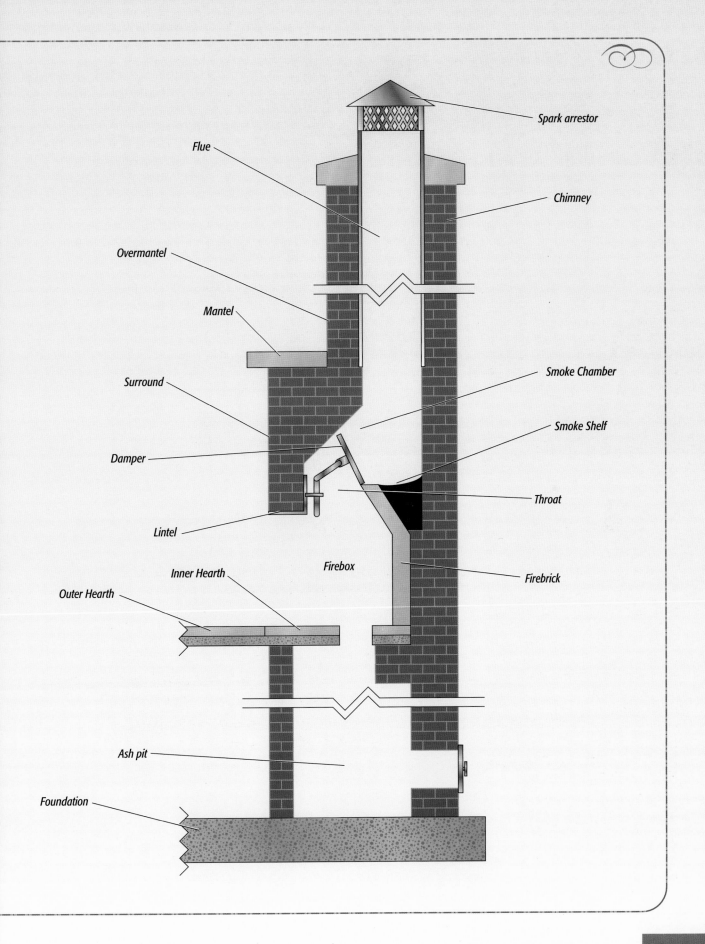

Spark arrestor

Flue

Chimney

Overmantel

Mantel

Smoke Chamber

Surround

Smoke Shelf

Damper

Throat

Lintel

Firebox

Firebrick

Inner Hearth

Outer Hearth

Ash pit

Foundation

European-style fireplaces—taller than they are wide—fit into small spaces that might not accommodate other types of fireplaces. This direct-vent gas fireplace is tucked between two large windows. Its campfire-style log set burns in a vertical pattern that fills the tall firebox.

The simple stone surround presents a clean, stylish face that suits this contemporary living room.

The geometric pattern in the tile surround and the herringbone pattern of the firebox brick were selected to complement the Arts and Crafts sensibilities of this cozy room. A rough stone hearth completes the picture.

The striking metal surround and square firebox draw attention despite their size.

A niche filled with logs makes the fireplace more realistic. The niche could also be used for other types of storage.

Raising the firebox gives it more emphasis within the room.

The modest log set is enhanced by accent lighting.

The capacity of a fireplace should be well matched to the room. Small rooms are best served by smaller fireplaces or by units that produce less heat. This direct vent fireplace has a shallow firebox and an electric ember bed. Its heat output is proportional to a smaller room.

Sealed wood-burning fireplaces

don't use indoor air for combustion, and they produce fewer combustion gases. The result is cleaner air indoors and out. Their technology means they burn less firewood than standard fireplaces, but they still produce abundant warmth.

Electric units answer the challenge of adding a fireplace to an urban apartment or condo. Their lightweight structure doesn't require a foundation— not even a reinforced floor in most cases—and installation involves little more than connecting the unit to the room's wiring.

Stepped ledges are reminiscent of the lovely wood steps leading to the room.

A metal flue leads to the chimney, which carries smoke and combustion gases out of the house.

Warming shelves provide a place to warm small items, such as mittens and hats.

Wood floors and direct access to the outdoors reduces the mess of bringing in wood for the fire.

A large stone hearth protects the wood floor from embers and sparks.

The masonry chimney behind this wood-burning stove creates a stylish backdrop, provides a vent for the fireplace, and radiates heat into the room.

A recessed light is positioned to wash the overmantel with light.

The overmantel tapers down to fit between the beams on the ceiling.

Alcoves on each side give the fireplace more prominence within the room.

The mantel legs are made of the same stone as the surround and the hearth, while the mantel is of a slightly different stone.

A French Provincial mantel surrounds a large firebox scaled to holds its own within the soaring room.

The specially-constructed firebox appears to be a seamless part of the fireplace.

A broad "mantel" projects slightly from the face of the surround.

A soaring concrete fireplace

and mantel create a dramatic backdrop

for this contemporary room.

The back of the shallow firebox is angled to control smoke and drafts.

A substantial concrete hearth, tinted black to provide contrast, provides a visual base for the sweeping gray feature.

DollarWise

Wood-burning fireplaces are romantic and beautiful, but absolutely not energy efficient. An open flue—even with a fire burning—is a giant hole sucking warmth from the house. One way to limit the heat loss of a wood-burning fireplace is to have glass doors installed over the fireplace. Even if you hire someone to do this for you, it won't take long for your energy savings to pay back your investment.

A standard fireplace becomes an important accessory when you add an interesting surround. This surround features a handful of hand painted tile within a field of less expensive field tile. By using a similar strategy, you can create a spectacular effect on less-than-spectacular budget.

This fireplace resonates with the dominant themes of the architecture without missing a beat—or an opportunity.

The stone overmantel is sized to fit into the window scheme, too.

The overmantel, mantel, and hearth are made of blocks of masonry that complement the modular scheme as well.

The square firebox is sized to fit into the modular design of the windows.

The hearth ledge also resembles the window trim.

Alcove window seats are made with the same material as the hearth and mantel.

Reflect on it.

Mirrors, brass, polished stone—reflective surfaces of any type—are at their best around firelight. They bounce welcome light and warmth into the room.

Silk shades direct light down to the reflective brass arms of the sconces.

There's even a reflection of sunlight in the painting over the mantel.

Polished marble reflects the warm glow of the flames.

Glass and brass doors brighten the scene.

Color, firelight, and polished surfaces warm the all-white background of this elegant living room.

The mirror above this vintage mantel and surround reflects the mantel arrangement, effectively doubling the impact of the simple objects.

The metal legs work well with the other metal accents in the room.

A glass coffee table doesn't compete for attention or visual space in the room.

A wood-burning fireplace encased in granite has a unique dimensional quality. The granite surround, with its inlaid mahogany accents, is further surrounded with mahogany trim. Soapstone appears in the hearth, the edge of the surround, and the mantel.

Mahogany accents the mantel and frames the fireplace surround.

Granite surround is inset with mahogany accents.

Soapstone forms the hearth and forms a border between the firebox and surround.

The ledges step in dimensions reminiscent of those that separate the ceiling beams.

Track lights are directed toward the marble surface.

A tall, narrow niche holds logs without demanding much attention.

Oversized brass andirons provide gleaming counterpoints against the expanse of marble.

Combined with a contemporary-style wood ceiling and traditional-style furnishings and accessories, this modern marble fireplace contributes nicely to the eclectic mix.

CHAPTER 3

Family Rooms & Great Rooms

J ust as "living room" is an inexact term, so are "family room" and "great room." The trouble is, there's no one word for these rooms. Whatever they're called, they're the rooms where we watch television, play games, listen to or play music, and simply "hang out." Great rooms typically are open to other rooms in the house, such as the kitchen and dining area.

Family rooms and great rooms are typically rather informal and comfortable, and they often prominently feature fireplaces. The shapes and materials used in these fireplaces are commonly chosen specifically with this informality in mind. These fireplaces also have to be designed with consideration for the other entertainment features in the room: they can't intrude upon space needed for pool tables or other game equipment, shouldn't be too close to space reserved for delicate electronics or musical instruments, and—in many cases—need to share the room's focus with a television.

Study the traffic patterns in your existing room or carefully study the blueprints for proposed rooms as you look at the following pages and consider the many options for a family room or recreation room fireplace.

When it comes to family rooms, location is everything. You want to be able to enjoy the fire as well as the entertainment features of the room—the television, electronics, and so forth—at the same time, if at all possible. And, you want to be able to do this from the comfort of your favorite sofa or chair. Accomplishing this can be a challenge.

The television fits into a niche in the cabinets, but its accessories (DVD player, cable box, and so forth) are hidden behind closed doors.

The chairs are positioned so the occupants can enjoy both the fire and the television.

The fireplace takes center

stage within a bank of cabinets that

hold the television and other electronics.

Light-colored, rough-cut stone stands out within the mellow tones of the surrounding cabinets.

The terra-cotta colored brick of the firebox contrasts beautifully with the light colored stone of the surround.

Cabinets such as these often house computers and other electronics, which works well as long as the electronics are not exposed to excessive heat. Consult owners' manuals before consigning delicate equipment to a space near the fireplace.

Clearances around a unit like this are carefully proscribed by building codes. Be sure to follow them carefully for your own safety and the safety of your home.

Musical instruments can be especially vulnerable to heat. Be sure to follow manufacturer's guidelines regarding placement in relationship to any source of heat.

Stoves must sit on top of non-combustible surfaces.

A cast-iron, wood-burning stove warms this music room.

A cultured stone surround wraps itself around the firebox.

Pool tables, especially custom built models, can be delicate. Consult your owners manual or retailer about suggestions about how close or far from the fireplace yours should be kept.

A high-top table and bar stools offer a wonderful place to have a fireside snack.

A flat screen television hangs on the overmantle above this gas fireplace, again creating one focus for both the television and fireplace.

A gas fireplace with a stunning stone surround is the centerpiece of an entertainment center tucked between two narrow windows. With the television sitting above the fireplace, each can be enjoyed from all angles of the sectional sofa.

This alcove is graced by both an "electronic hearth," as television is sometimes called, and the hearth of a beautiful gas fireplace. The television is tucked beneath an extension of the breakfast bar, which acts as a mantel. The fireplace is surrounded by a smooth stone surface uninterrupted by a mantel or any other accessories.

(left) The bay-window shaped glass front on this gas fireplace allows the homeowners to see the fire from the front or from either side of the fireplace. It is especially pleasant to play the piano while enjoying the fire.

This beautiful stone fireplace sits in a niche that the family uses for games, reading, and other quiet activities. Built-in benches on either side of the space hold their blankets and pillows as well as their favorite games and other toys.

Cast-iron doors and ceramic glass doors provide a wide view of the fire.

An enormous wood-burning fireplace is centered along one wall of this recreation room, and the television is centered along the adjacent wall. The homeowners solved the perennial question of which way to look by adding a curved sofa that allows them the luxury of enjoying both. Placing the pool table at the end of the room allows players to see both the television and the fire, as well.

Insulated glass and modern construction methods make a sunroom comfortable in any weather.

Masonry surfaces radiate heat into the room on all sides.

The large firebox lets the family burn larger logs than standard fireboxes.

The raised hearth is covered with ceramic tile that matches the border on the flue extension.

Lightweight chairs can be drawn closer to the fire on chilly days.

The family room of this lake-front cottage wraps around a large, free-standing fireplace. The fireplace is the heart of the entire house, and its flue, which rises nearly unadorned to the ceiling, melds into the room's architecture.

This white brick surrounding this fireplace extends along the adjacent wall, creating a point of interest for the entire room. While the fireplace in undeniably the focus of the room, the large armoire holds another: the television. Electronics of all sorts can be hidden behind the closed doors of armoires and cabinets, and open for viewing only when they're being used.

The theme of this great room seems to be "bigger is better." In a room this large, filled with pieces of this scale, only a dramatic fireplace could hold its own. The stone wall topped by massive logs is more than up for the task. Topped by oversized vases filled with branches and an enormous tapestry, the fireplace anchors a cozy corner in the middle of all this space.

Overstuffed sofas and chairs flank an oversized stone fireplace in this elegant family room. A pool table sits behind the central seating area, ready for all comers.

Realistic gas logs fill the firebox.

A relatively small but nicely detailed mantel hangs in the center of the fireplace.

Richly detailed paneling covers the overmantel, linking it to the bookcases and wall paneling.

The family room becomes a home theatre when the viewing screen and projector are lowered from their hiding places.

Simple black lanterns glow above the mantel.

A custom-built fire screen and large andirons guard the unique firebox.

Fireplace chairs are built lower to the ground so that one can enjoy the warmth close at hand.

Cathedral-style arches grace the fireplace surround, display niches, and china cabinet.

Everything about this room is great: the rich pine paneling and gorgeous coordinated mantel, the cathedral-arched display niches and fireplace surround, the oversized cast-iron andirons and electric lanterns, and the generous coffee table/ottoman.

Gather round the fire.

As if its stature and materials weren't enough to draw attention, the beams radiating out from the stone chimney direct all eyes to the unique stone wall and fireplace.

The irregular shape of this massive stone fireplace provides an interesting counterpoint to the tightly structured architecture of the room.

Heat generated by the wood-burning stove is absorbed and radiated into the room by the brick hearth and wall. Openings in the brick wall allow warmth to circulate to the rear, too.

The gentle curve of the hearth softens the many straight lines of the room.

Your home may be much newer than this rustic cabin, but if you love the look of vintage objects and antiques, work them into your fireplace. Here, vintage corbels support a mantel made of reclaimed lumber.

This fireplace was built from hand-gathered stones smoothed by water. Gathering your own stones for construction might be an option for you, too.

The large river stone fireplace
is the centerpiece of this 1900s log cabin.

Vintage collectibles cover the mantel.

The river stone extends onto the hearth.

A recessed niche brings the perceived height of the fireplace up to equal that of the cabinets.

Raising the firebox makes it more prominent within the room.

A raised fireplace is snuggled between built-in cabinets that rest beneath curved clerestory windows. In relationship to the windows and cabinets, the fireplace is rather small, but dark colors and brass accents give it enough mass to create visual balance.

The stone of the fireplace extends along the wall and floor, creating a focal point for the room. The overmantel tapers down as it rises toward the ceiling, giving the fireplace its own shape despite the extension of the stone.

A rough-hewn log acts as a mantel and display ledge. Its weathered colors are a perfect complement to the stone of the fireplace.

Rustic doors with strap hinges cover an area where electronics and other entertainment devices are stored.

Boulders are used as benches on each side of the fireplace.

Repeating a design theme is an easy way to link the fireplace to the room. The tile on the surround and hearth were sized to duplicate the effect of the leaded glass window to the left of the fireplace, and the mantel and surround were designed to resemble the window's trim.

CHAPTER 4

Bedrooms

The bedroom may not be the first place you think of to add a fireplace, but for most people, it's a very strong second. In fact, according to the Hearth, Patio, and Barbeque Association, the master bedroom is the most desired location for a second fireplace. Whether you want to fan the flames of romance or simply enjoy the warmth and ambience of a fire while you snuggle under the covers, a fireplace may be the answer.

Planning is critical when adding a fireplace to a bedroom because local building codes are especially exacting when it comes to fireplaces in bedrooms. The potentially-dangerous combination of burning fires and sleeping people is not taken lightly by most municipalities, so do your homework. In some communites, self-venting fireplaces are not allowed. Before you commit to a bedroom fireplace project, talk with a local building inspector and check with your insurance agent. You need to know exactly what is involved in order to calculate the true cost of your project.

Properly planned and installed, bedroom fireplaces are perfectly safe and enjoyable. As with any fireplace project, protect yourself and your family by applying for all necessary permits and submitting to each requested inspection.

Sweets for the suite.

A simple shelf mantel is well matched with the room's other trim work.

Subtle hand-painted tiles produce an interesting surround that complements the room rather than dominating it.

The firebox is raised so the homeowners can enjoy the fire while reclining on the bed.

An ottoman can be rolled in front of the fire when you want a front-row seat and away from the heat when you don't.

A ceiling fan drives the rising heat from the fireplace down into the room where you can enjoy it.

Recessed lights highlight the fireplace area.

A raised fireplace

warms this bedroom both literally and figuratively. The room is saved from dullness by the play of angles and small touches of color in the furnishings and on the fireplace surround. The designers took advantage of the shape and height of the ceilings as well as the space around the fireplace to create architectural interest in this cheerful, airy room.

When shopping for a fireplace for a bedroom, consider how you'll use it and try to find features that work for you. For instance, some electric and gas fireplaces come equipped with programmable timers that start and extinguish the fire at preset times, which lets you wake to a warm, cheerful room and eliminates the need to turn off the fire before you drift off to sleep.

If you choose a gas fireplace for your bedroom, look for one that doesn't need electricity to operate or one that has a back-up battery. Come the first winter power outage, you'll sleep warm no matter how cruel the temperature or deep the snow.

High-quality firebrick looks like traditional masonry.

Located on a short, angled wall, the fireplace creates a focal point for the room.

A raised fireplace doesn't require a front hearth if space is tight.

This smaller gas fireplace suits the scale of a bedroom, and the simple marble surround blends into the décor without a hitch. Its raised firebox is positioned for viewing from the bed.

A portable electric stove adds period charm to a Colonial-style bedroom. Electric stoves are approved for bedrooms in virtually all municipalities, and they're well suited to many climates. Most can be adjusted to provide the ambience of flames without warmth or to provide both flames and warmth.

An antique Swedish wood-burning stove, known as a kakelugnar, rounds out the corner of this bedroom. Small stoves, such as this or more modern versions, can be fit into surprisingly small spaces.

The "stepped" design of the wall provides shelves for objet d'art.

A see-through gas fireplace does double duty between the sleeping and seating area in this small home.

There is no front hearth to interrupt the flow of the space. With a sealed insert or electric fireplace, this is allowed in most areas, but check your local building codes.

The fireplace wall forms a barrier between sleeping and seating areas.

The tall fireplace surround and mantel bring the high ceiling and large room into a more human scale. Also, the candlestick and artwork over the mantel fill the massive wall space with color and texture.

Coordinate the fireplace with the room.

The fireplace appears to be a natural part of the whole rather than an afterthought. In this case, the spare stone surround and geometric mantel and hearth reflect the sensibility of the cabinet doors and window trim as well as the color scheme.

The neutral color scheme, simple stone surround, and picture-frame details on the mantel blend the fireplace into the design of this spacious bedroom.

A simple metal fire screen suspended from the top of the firebox protects the room from sparks without obscuring the fire.

The style of the mantel reflects the style of the dresser and other elements of the room.

The firebox on this fireplace is taller than it is wide, in perfect keeping with the dimensions and design of the Craftsman-style bedroom.

The joinery of the face of the mantel reflects the joinery used on the doorframes and cabinets.

The mantel is topped with a symmetrical arrangement of family photos and sentimental objects.

The bias-relief tile surround is true to the style of fireplace and the room.

Most of us decorate the public spaces of our homes for the seasons and holidays because those are shared spaces, places where we expect to entertain others. Decorating a bedroom for the seasons and holidays is a more personal, intimate gesture, one that signals a choice to treat ourselves as graciously as we treat our guests. If you want to start small, try decorating the mantel over the bedroom fireplace.

Backed by framed needlework, this collection of Santas and antique German belsnickels (fur Nicholas) makes the mantel the focal point of the room.

Boxwood, evergreens, fruit, and cranberry strings grace this New England-style mantel. A note of caution: Be very careful when using live greenery. Don't drape it too close to the firebox and discard it before it's dry enough to become a safety hazard. And, of course, never leave a fire burning unattended.

Match the scale of your decorations to the scale of the room. When decorating a mantel, large items draw focus where small ones can disappear or look more like clutter than decorations.

Hanging at an angle, these swamp skis balance the mass of the large gas fireplace and open rafters. With their visual weight in place, the decorator was free to fill in with a little natural greenery and several smaller objects.

A white mantel against a rich color of paint creates visual pop, even to neutral color schemes.

A bank of white candles and white twinkle lights glow against neutral backgrounds.

Candle sconces and a picture-frame light add light and warmth to the area, even when the fire isn't burning.

Symmetry and subtle color contrasts are repeated throughout this bedroom. The colors of the fireplace, with its taupeish-gray surround and white mantel, continue through the furnishings and linens. The undulations of the fire ripple through the curves of the built-ins, the texture of the carpet—even the curves of the chairs and the lace-trimmed edges of the draperies. These curves are neatly offset by the straight lines of the bedposts, the rectilinear lines of the bench, and the strictly symmetrical arrangement of objects over the mantel.

*Dollar*Wise

Adding a fireplace to a bedroom can be a fairly expensive project. If you're not sure you'll be staying in your home long enough to justify the expense, consider a portable electric fireplace or stove. These appliances simply plug into the wall and can be moved from room to room quite easily. They don't require any installation or construction (you don't even need a building permit to install one) and can be moved with you to a new home when the time comes.

The ornate surround on this gas fireplace is a strong design feature all year long. The elaborate texture of the surround is balanced by the clean lines of a symmetrical arrangement of muted prints matted with soft ivory and framed with simple molding.

If space is tight, go stand in the corner.

Corner fireplaces often have smaller footprints and use less room space than other styles. If space is an issue in your bedroom, look into the corners.

This kiva-style fireplace fits into the corner of the bedroom like a goose-down pillow into a high-thread-count pillowcase. It suits the room and fills the space without overpowering it. By keeping the texture and color the same as the surrounding walls, the homeowners made the most of the space available.

This gas fireplace is designed to add more than just warmth and flames. It stands atop a corner shelf that can be used to display books or interesting objects of any kind. Models are also available with drawers, wine racks, and so forth.

If painting or stenciling is one of your talents, use it to personalize your project.

Alternating two strong colors of tiles costs no more than using one color.

With its black-and-white tile and hand painted design, this corner fireplace is a showstopper. Its angles and planes were clearly designed by someone who thinks "outside the box," as was the diagonal hardwood floor and the nearby built-in bench. Before committing to a humdrum plan, consider how to spice up the design without spending a fortune.

Concrete, a surprisingly adaptable material, is not just for sidewalks anymore. It can be tinted, polished, and formed into remarkable shapes. Here, an angled column establishes strong lines for a decidedly contemporary bedroom. A concrete fireplace like this one is not an inexpensive choice, but it is a spectacular one.

Concrete is heavy and often requires special structural support for the floors supporting the fireplace.

Repeating the ceramic tile from the adjacent bathroom floor creates a nice transition from room to room.

Multi-sided fireplaces offer a view of the flames from many angles. In this bedroom, the bathing area is open to the sitting and sleeping areas, and the wood-burning, bay-shaped fireplace can be enjoyed from each.

CHAPTER 5

Kitchens & Dining Areas

Once upon a time, it was the hearth that made the kitchen the heart of the home, but as modern appliances made their way into kitchens, fireplaces gravitated out of them. Today, homeowners want their kitchens to serve more roles than ever: cooking area, dining space, home office, and entertainment center, among them. More and more frequently, that means adding a fireplace in this, the most quintessential of gathering places.

Choosing a fireplace for a kitchen or dining area is more than a matter of taste. Cleanliness, ease of use, and fuel choices are possibly more important here than in any other room of the house. Do you really want wood stacked or coal sitting out near a dining or food preparation area? Would corn or pellets be practical? Will the fireplace or stove be a source of auxiliary heat or will it be more for ambience? Ask yourself these and other questions as you look through the fireplaces in this chapter and evaluate your choices.

The side of the fireplace extends beyond the food prep area, shielding it from smoke and ashes.

A multi-sided fireplace presents views from several areas of the room.

A niche beneath the firebox provides storage space for fire logs.

A fire glows in the heart of this home.

The stainless steel range hood is expanded to form a hood for the fireplace.

The ceramic tile floor is easy to clean, non-flammable, and resistant to damage from sparks.

Gleaming stainless steel and used brick fold a pier-style fireplace into the rustic style of this log home.

A fireplace for all reasons, this custom-designed, multi-sided fireplace offers something to every part of the room.

Sturdy wood grips on the racks make them easier to handle.

Long-handled utensils stand ready to adjust the fire.

An open-fire grill faces the kitchen.
A deep firebox and movable racks make this an ideal place to warm, toast, grill, or fire-roast a meal.

A large niche holds stacks of firewood nearby.

A cast-iron stove offers old-fashioned ambience as well as a constant source of warmth on cold days.

A wide masonry hearth protects the nearby hardwood floor from flying sparks and falling embers.

A massive masonry structure, such as this, requires substantial structural support and careful engineering.

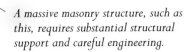

The curved hearth and rounded edges of the mantel soften the severity of the otherwise angular construction.

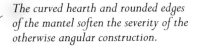

A magnificently proportioned fireplace faces the seating area.

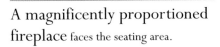

The size, shape, and color of the massive fireplace set the tone for this great room as well as the areas beyond. Gray stone tiles cover the entire structure—chimney, surround, mantel, and hearth. Surrounded, as it is, by wood tones and white, fireplace dominates the room. Its severe lines and color are continued in the cabinets, countertops, and furnishings.

A simple wood mantel tops the fireplace.

The raised firebox can be seen over the countertops and from the dining area beyond.

Accessories contribute to the illusion when a fireplace is gas or electric.

In contrast to the fireplace in the photo above, this fireplace recedes into background while other design elements take center stage.

Light from halogen spots play across the polished surface of the concrete surround and hearth.

This kitchen is warmed by a haphazard looking brick chimney and a concrete fireplace that is a model of symmetry.

Curves integrate the sway-backed chimney into the straight lines of the surround and mantel.

The firebox, taller than it is wide, completes the illusion of the chimney sweeping down to the fireplace.

Gleaming ceramic tile covers this wood-burning stove,
which has solid brass doors. Although you can't see the fire, you can feel its
warmth radiated by the tile and smell its pleasant aroma. The tile-clad wall
behind the stove also radiates warmth and shields the framing from damage.

A stone alcove radiates the heat of this wood-burning stove into the kitchen and nearby dining area. The black countertops help integrate the vent pipe, which rises to the roof without any camouflage or decoration.

This particular stove has an ash drawer and a niche for logs. When choosing a wood-burning stove, especially for a kitchen, make sure it's easy to load and easy to clean.

The curved glass door offers a large viewing area relative to the size of the stove.

An ash drawer makes it easier to clean out the stove.

Logs are stored in the convenient niche.

Generations of Scandinavians have warmed their homes with wood-burning soapstone fire-places. These days, they export similar products, all over the world, to discriminating homeowners who want environmentally responsible, wood-burning fireplaces and stoves. The virtue of these products is, according to several manufacturers, soapstone's unique ability to retain and radiate heat, which is approximately twice that of ordinary masonry brick. One manufacturer claims that two armloads of wood will heat an average home for 12 to 24 hours—long after the fire has burned out. Even remembering that the average Scandinavian home is much smaller than the average North American home, that statistic indicates the superior performance of soap-stone stoves and fireplaces. These products typically are expensive, but their outstanding performance and good looks may make them worth the investment for you.

Most soapstone stoves and fireplaces have to be hand built on the site. As with any masonry fireplace, they require a substantial foundation and support.

A wide soapstone hearth protects the kitchen floor.

This soapstone stove warms the kitchen and can be used for baking, too. The oven is especially good for baking for pastries and breads. Standing in the middle of the kitchen, warm air is able to radiate from all directions and circulate efficiently.

This soapstone stove is used for both cooking and baking as well as heating the kitchen. Although it might not be practical for everyday living, such an arrangement could be delightful in a rural or vacation home, especially in remote locations where power failures are common during severe weather.

Soapstone tile behind the stove adds to its ability to retain and radiate heat.

This wooden paddle is used to slide baked goods in and out of the oven.

The heat from this beautiful soapstone stove and hearth radiates out to the ceramic tile, warming the kitchen floor as well as the rest of the area.

The large firebox of the
gas fireplace creates a view
from many angles in this cozy dining
room. The contrast of the narrow
black brick surround against the
white mantel makes the fireplace
seem even larger. Local codes are
very specific about separating the
firebox from combustible materials,
so be sure to check the regulations
and plan accordingly.

This see-through gas fireplace shares the luxury between the dining room and adjoining
kitchen, a thoroughly pleasant arrangement. See-through fireplaces give you twice the opportunities to enjoy the fireplace without investing in two separate units. Once upon a time, see-through
fireplaces were considered troublesome, but today's versions are both elegant and efficient.

Share the wealth.

A pier fireplace between the kitchen and family room offers a view of the flames from each. As shown here, pier fireplaces typically offer views from three sides. This particular gas fireplace has a nearly invisible smoke shield and fine mesh screen to enhance the view of the flames.

The fireplace equivalent of surround-sound, these fireplaces share a flue and chimney, but not one hearth and damper. The fires can be built independently of one another, but just imagine how charming it would be to live among a full panorama of flames. Again, this would be a fairly expensive project, and only you can judge its worth for your home.

Set into a tile wall, this arched gas fireplace creates
the illusion of an old-fashioned wood-burning oven,
but it comes without the mess or trouble of maintaining a wood fire. The
narrow brass trim on the firebox was designed for a contemporary or
Mission-style kitchen but would look equally stunning with many styles.

Glass doors can reach extreme temperatures when exposed to roaring fires. Don't touch the glass itself—use the handles—and protect young children from touching or bumping into it.

Positioned almost dead center in the room, this large brick fireplace provides the backdrop for a breakfast bar, a display area for antiques, and a marble hearth-bench where family and guests can take in the proceedings. If you have the space for it, a fireplace like this can become the feature attraction of the kitchen.

When is a fireplace more than a fireplace? When it includes built-in furnishings, such as this handsome wine rack. Even when space is limited, a raised corner fireplace can be tucked into a kitchen or dining room with a minimum of trouble and expense.

Centered between two broad sets of windows, this fireplace is tall and wide enough to be enjoyed from any corner of the room. If the homeowners had chosen a fireplace of more standard proportions, it might have been hidden from view by tall chairs in the seating area. A high grate and campfire-style fire add height to the flames, as well. When planning a fireplace for a kitchen, dining area, or great room, consider all the angles of the room, not just the most obvious.

The narrow proportions of this dining area/library
dictated at least a fairly modest size, but the homeowners wanted a
fireplace with substantial presence. They achieved their goals by tailor-
ing the fireplace wall and mantel to the room's dimensions and by
adding a custom designed tile surround with a colorful leaf motif.

*Sealed glass doors are a must when
there is no hearth, especially in a
room overflowing with flammable
materials, such as these books.*

*An angled wall helps the fire-
place fit into the narrow room.*

*Wrapping the mantle around
the sides of the fireplace added
display space without gobbling
up a lot of territory.*

*A simple design in strong
colors makes a statement
without becoming cluttered.*

CHAPTER 6

Outdoor Rooms

The hottest trend in landscaping is the outdoor room, an idea whose time has undeniably come. Today's outdoor rooms are delineated by floors (decks and patios), walls (fences and other walls), ceilings (trellises and arbors), and include furnishings. More and more often, outdoor rooms are being created around outdoor fireplaces. It's a natural choice. After all, indoors or out, people are naturally drawn to the light and warmth of a fire.

The choices for outdoor fireplaces are much the same as for indoor models. You can build a masonry fireplace and chimney, which can be fairly expensive because, even outdoors, the weight of these structures requires footings. Lightweight prefab wood-burning and gas fireplaces are manufactured for outdoor settings—some with exhaust vents so they don't even require chimneys. Finally, the least expensive, most flexible options are freestanding wood-burning or gas fire pits.

Unless you live in a remote location, you share the great outdoors with neighbors, and it's important to be considerate when planning outdoor additions. As much as possible, make sure the smoke will not drift directly into neighbors' windows, that the center of your gatherings won't be too close to their bedrooms, and that the heat and smoke won't damage trees and shrubbery—including your own.

As you look through the following pages and consider various options, keep in mind the style of your home, the size of your yard, and your goals for the fireplace.

The chimney on an outdoor fireplace should be equipped with a spark arrestor.

Local building codes dictate clearances between a fireplace and combustible materials, such as these beams.

A roaring fire warms the broad porch in front of this home while another serves the gathering space indoors.

Heat-resistant siding, such as this brick, is critical if the fireplace adjoins or is close to the house.

A tall, wide firebox provides room for roaring fires.

Burn only dry, seasoned wood, even in an outdoor fireplace. Green wood produces more creosote and makes it necessary to clean the chimney more frequently.

A concrete or masonry surface is ideal for the floor in front of a fireplace.

Natural stone tiles are used for the indoor floor, the outdoor patio surface, and the fireplace surround.

A non-venting gas firelog set allows for walls inset with glass windows above the fireplace.

Well-sealed doors, both inside and outside, make the fireplace as weather-tight as an energy-efficient window.

A see-through gas insert is a beautiful option for an indoor/outdoor fireplace. The stainless steel frame of this fireplace is weatherproof, and the doors are sealed with a sheet of tempered glass covering the outside face. Equipped in this way, the fireplace can be enjoyed in any weather.

Set into a bank of glass, this indoor/outdoor, see-through fireplace is a design marvel. From either side the fireplace seems to float in space, especially at night when the windows are dark.

The warmth of the fire radiates through the entire masonry pool deck, keeping it comfortable on chilly desert nights.

One can snuggle up to the warmth of the fire

or luxuriate in the warm waters of the spa. But why choose one

or the other when you can have both? A kiva-style fireplace

opens to the spa area as well as the dining area beyond.

*A non-combustible masonry
wall topped by a metal fence
separates the fireplace and spa
from the desert landscape.*

*A patio umbrella shades
the dining space on the
other side of the fireplace.*

*Massive urns on pedestals keep
bathers from accidentally getting too close to hot surfaces.*

*Good lighting completes
the transformation into
an outdoor room.*

For those who prefer a chimney for their fireplace, there are plenty of options available. This particular fireplace ships as a wood-burning unit, although it can easily be converted to gas. The stainless steel unit is weatherproof, as is the brick refractory. Installed in a stone surround, it lights up the landscape.

Gas fireplaces are just as convenient and easy to use in outdoor rooms as they are interior spaces, and manufacturers now produce special outdoor units. This gas fireplace is vented through the decorative front grill, which eliminates the need for a chimney and reduces the expense of installing the fireplace. The concrete log set and refractory are completely weatherproof.

Not all outdoor rooms are found on suburban lawns and rural lots. City dwellers enjoy dining al fresco by firelight as much as the next person, but until recently it was impractical at best. Now there are gas fireplaces that can be installed anywhere, including a rooftop or terrace. If this is your heart's desire, consult a local building inspector and your retailer or contractor for suggestions. Not all outdoor units are approved for this type of use, but there are plenty of available options if you shop wisely.

In a wooded area such as this, fire safety is critical.

A broad edge puts a little distance between the center of the pit and the seating area.

Brick—selected to complement the house—makes a non-combustible floor for the area.

Non-combustible metal supports the bench surrounding the pit.

Firepits are another attractive option for lighting up the back yard. This circular version was custom built to complement the brick Tudor home and wood deck.

Not everyone has a huge budget or a huge yard, for that matter. And wood-burning fire pits are not allowed in all communities. Still, those realities don't eliminate the possibility of gathering around the flames under a starry sky. In such situations, a cast-iron fire base may be the perfect answer. These units, which are available for either natural gas or propane, operate with a simple on/off switch and are approved for use on wood decks, stone or brick patios, and concrete.

For a more integrated look, you can buy a burner unit and build a stone surround, such as the ledge stone surround here. Make sure to allow for the necessary clearances, which in most communities means at least 16 inches of free space all the way around the pit and at least 7 feet from the top of the unit.

CHAPTER 7

Decorating Fireplaces

A fireplace becomes the focal point of almost any room, which presents both challenges and opportunities. First, the challenges: Unadorned, many mantels look as though something's missing, and there are the perennial questions of what to use and how to arrange it and how much is too much. The good news is that there really are no wrong answers, and all the right answers lie within you.

Now, the opportunities: fireplaces and mantels give you a place to play with color and texture and ideas. Because arrangements can be changed with the seasons or your mood, your decisions aren't fraught with tension. If you come up with a wild idea, try it. If it doesn't work, you can easily change it.

Another great thing about mantels is that they're great places to showcase collections. Art work, photos, dolls—you name it, and you can create a dazzling display with it as long as you apply a little imagination and ingenuity. One note of caution: Your collection will be exposed to heat when you use the fireplace. This might not be the best place to display some antiques and fragile pieces.

As you look through the following pages, think about your room, your special possessions, and what you want your fireplace to say about your home and you.

DECORATING FIREPLACES

Taking its cues from the room's architecture and furnishings, this arrangement emphasizes all its best features.

Spikes of greenery are just enough to liven up the symmetrical grouping without overpowering it.

Pieces from the owners' cherished collection of blue-and-white pottery complete the scene.

The billowing sails in the painting echo the soaring ceiling above the doors.

The dark mantel appears to be a natural extension of the room's paneling and the marble surround stands out without shouting to be noticed.

A brass fender and andirons carry just the right note of formality for the room.

A baroque white mantel surrounds this fireplace with the feeling of artful luxury. Black wrought-iron accessories ground the fanciful mantel and help it seem all of a piece with the simple terra-cotta tile hearth. If you would like to find an antique mantel for your fireplace, measure it carefully and carry the dimensions with you at all times. You never know when you might run across a possibility in your travels, and you wouldn't want to let the right one get away because you weren't sure it would fit.

The glass-block hearth and stone gargoyle set the tone in this unique fireside vignette. Hand-forged fire tools hold their own in this setting, as does the hand thrown pot that holds kindling at the ready.

*Dollar*Wise

A fireback, a decorative cast-iron panel, increases the heat output of a fireplace by absorbing heat and radiating it back into the room. They also protect the bricks in the back of the firebox from smoke and soot. Antique and vintage firebacks are highly sought after and can be expensive. Good reproductions can be found at more reasonable prices.

A concrete shelf provides a hearth-cum-bench for this raised fireplace as well as a sturdy floor for the wood storage area tucked behind the fireplace wall. With the simplicity of the structure and dramatic lighting, subtle touches are all that's needed to complete this scene.

A hand painted faux finish on the wood floor adjoining the hearth creates eye-popping interest. Use paint to emphasize features you especially appreciate. It's inexpensive and easy to do.

Architectural salvage frames an unused fieldstone fireplace. The white columns flanking the stone give the room a visual lift while other, more delicate, pieces integrate the massive stone into the more feminine feeling of the room.

Potted geraniums fill the firebox of this unused fireplace. The mottled tones of the faux painting on the walls creates the golden feeling of warmth despite the absence of a fire.

A salvaged mantel embraces a vintage stove front to create a credible illusion of a fireplace against a dramatic red wall.

This fireplace has really gone to the dogs. Not literally of course, but the whimsical, dog-bone festooned garland makes it clear that this is a place to have fun. Filling the firebox with artificial greenery and twinkling lights creates a warm glow and still allows you to hang your stockings from the chimney with care. (Never hang flammable materials within range of real flames.)

Resource Guide

A listing of resources for information, designs, and products found in IdeaWise Fireplaces.

Introduction

page 8
Fireplace by
Heat & Glo
888-427-3973
www.heatnglo.com

page 9
Gas stove by
Quadra-Fire
800-926-4356
www.quadrafire.com

Page 10
Soapstone Fireplace by
Tulikivi
+358 (0)207 636 000
www.tulikivi.com

Options

Page 16 (both)
Fireplace by
Vermont Castings CFM Corporation
905-858-8010
www.cfmcorp.com

page 17 (top)
Traditional Fireplace by
Heat & Glo
888-427-3973
www.heatnglo.com

Page 17 (bottom left)
Zero Clearance Fireplace by
Fuego Flame Fireplaces
800-445-1867
www.fuegoflame.com

Pages 17 (bottom right), 18
Gas insert and stove by
Quadra-Fire
800-926-4356
www.quadrafire.com

Page 26
Firebox by
Heat & Glo
888-427-3973
www.heatnglo.com

Living Rooms

Page 33 (top)
Gas Fireplace by
Quadra-Fire
800-926-4356
www.quadrafire.com

pages 38 (top), 39
Wood-burning stoves by
Quadra-Fire
800-926-4356
www.quadrafire.com

page 40
Electric Insert by
Heat & Glo
888-427-3973
www.heatnglo.com

Pages 44 (top), 45
Small fireboxes by
Heat & Glo
888-427-3973
www.heatnglo.com

page 46 (top)
Wood-burning fireplace by
Vermont Castings
CFM Corporation
905-858-8010
www.cfmcorp.com

page 46 (bottom)
Electric Fireplace by
Heat & Glo
888-427-3973
www.heatnglo.com

page 49
Concrete fireplace by
Buddy Rhodes for Designer Ruth
Saferenko & Associates and Rupel,
Geiser & McLeod Architects
www.buddyrhodes.com

page 51
fireplace design by
Walter Moberg
Moberg Fireplaces, Inc.
503-227-0547
www.mobergfireplaces.com

page 54 (top)
Fireplace design by
Walter Moberg
Moberg Fireplaces, Inc.
503-227-0547
www.mobergfireplaces.com

page 54 (bottom)
Gas fireplace insert by
Vermont Castings
CFM Corporation
905-858-8010
www.cfmcorp.com

Resource Guide

(continued)

Family Rooms and Great Rooms

Fireplace design by
Walter Moberg
Moberg Fireplaces, Inc.
503-227-0547
www.mobergfireplaces.com

page 61 (top)
Stone Fireplace by
Heat & Glo
888-427-3973
www.heatnglo.com

page 62 (both)
Gas and Electric Fireplaces by
Quadra-Fire
800-926-4356
www.quadrafire.com

page 63
Cast iron fireplace by
Vermont Castings
CFM Corporation
905-858-8010
www.cfmcorp.com

Bedrooms

page 82
Gas fireplace by
Heat & Glo
888-427-3973
www.heatnglo.com

page 83 (top)
Portable electric stove by
Quadra-Fire
800-926-4356
www.quadrafire.com

page 93
Built-in Gas Fireplace by
Heat & Glo
888-427-3973
www.heatnglo.com

page 95
Multi-sided fireplace by
Heat & Glo
888-427-3973
www.heatnglo.com

Resource Guide

(continued)

Kitchens and Dining Areas

page 96
Soapstone woodburning stove by
Tulikivi
+358 (0)207 636 000
www.tulikivi.com

page 103
Concrete Fireplace by
Jim Scott for Buddy Rhodes.
www.buddyrhodes.com

pages 106-107
Soapstone woodburning ovens by
Tulikivi
+358 (0)207 636 000
www.tulikivi.com

pages 108 (bottom) and 109 (top)
Dining area fireplaces by
Heat & Glo
888-427-3973
www.heatnglo.com

page 110
Gas kitchen fireplace by
Heat & Glo
888-427-3973
www.heatnglo.com

Page 111 (bottom)
Built-in fireplace by
Heat & Glo
888-427-3973
www.heatnglo.com

Outdoor Rooms

page 118
Indoor/outdoor fireplace by
Vermont Castings
CFM Corporation
905-858-8010
www.cfmcorp.com

page 119
Indoor/outdoor fireplace by
Heat & Glo
888-427-3973
www.heatnglo.com

pages 120-121
Outdoor fireplaces by
California Pools and Spas
626-974-9417
www.californiapools.com

page 122 (both)
Outdoor fireplaces by
Heat & Glo
888-427-3973
www.heatnglo.com

page123
Outdoor gas fireplace by
Vermont Castings
CFM Corporation
905-858-8010
www.cfmcorp.com

pages 124 (bottom) and 125
Outdoor fireplaces by
Vermont Castings
CFM Corporation
905-858-8010
www.cfmcorp.com

Photo Credits

Front cover and title page: Photo courtesy of Tulikivi. Back cover: (top left) ©Getty Images/Royalty-free; (top right and center) photos courtesy of Heat-N-Glo; (bottom left) photo courtesy of Quadra-Fire; (bottom right) California Pools and Spas.

p. 2: ©Getty Images/Royalty Free.

p. 3: (bottom left) Photo courtesy of Buddy Rhodes/for Ruth Soferenko & Associates and Rupel Geiser & Mcleod Architects; (bottom right) Brand X Pictures/Royalty free.

p. 4-5: ©Brian Vanden Brink.

pp. 6-7: (both) Brian Vanden Brink.

p. 8: Photo courtesy of Heat-N-Glo.

p. 9: Photo courtesy of Quadra-Fire.

p. 10: (top) Photo courtesy of Tulikivi; (bottom) ©Brand X Pictures/Royalty Free.

p. 12: ©Getty Images/Royalty free.

p. 15: ©Brian Vanden Brink.

p. 16: Photo courtesy of Vermont Castings.

p. 17: (top) Photo courtesy of Heat-N-Glo; (bottom left) Photo courtesy of Fuego Flame; (bottom right) Photo courtesy of Quadra-Fire.

p. 18: Photo courtesy of Quadra-Fire.

p. 19: ©www.davidduncanlivingston.com.

p. 26: Photo courtesy of Heat-N-Glo.

p. 28: ©Brian Vanden Brink.

p. 30-31: ©www.davidduncanlivingston.com.

p. 32: ©Jessie Walker.

p.33: (top) Photo courtesy of Quadra-Fire; (bottom) ©Jessie Walker.

p.34: ©Jessie Walker.

p. 35:©Brand X Pictures/Royalty Free.

p. 36: ©www.davidduncanlivingston.com.

p. 37: ©Brand X Pictures/Royalty Free.

p. 38: (top) Photo courtesy of Quadra-Fire; (bottom) ©Jessie Walker.

p. 39: Photo courtesy of Quadra-Fire.

p. 40: Photo courtesy of Heat-N-Glo.

p. 41: ©Brian Vanden Brink.

p. 44: (top) Photo courtesy of Heat-N-Glo; (bottom) ©Brian Vanden Brink.

p. 45: Photo courtesy of Heat-N-Glo.

p. 46: Photo courtesy of Vermont Castings.

p. 47: ©Brian Vanden Brink.

p. 48: ©www.davidduncanlivingston.com

p. 49: Photo courtesy of Buddy Rhodes for Ruth Soferenko & Associates and Rupel Geiser & McLeod Architects.

p. 50: ©Jessie Walker.

p. 51: Photo courtesy of Walter Mober Designs.

p. 52: ©Brian Vanden Brink.

p. 53: ©Jessie Walker.

p. 54: (top) Photo courtesy of Walter Moberg Designs; (bottom) Photo courtesy of Vermont Castings.

p. 55: ©Jessie Walker.

p. 56: Photo courtesy of Walter Moberg Designs.

pp. 58-59: ©Brian Vanden Brink.

p. 60: ©Jessie Walker.

p. 61: (top) Photo courtesy of Heat-N-Glo; (bottom) ©www.davidduncanlivingston.com.

p. 62: (both) Photo courtesy of Quadra-Fire.

p. 63: ©Photo courtesy of Vermont Castings.

p. 64: ©Brian Vanden Brink.

p. 66: ©Jessie Walker.

p. 67: (top) ©Jessie Walker; Getty Images/Royalty Free.

pp. 68-73: ©Brian Vanden Brink.

pp. 74-76: ©Jessie Walker.

p. 77: ©www.davidduncanlivingston.com.

p. 78: ©Andrea Rugg.

pp. 80-81: ©Jessie Walker.

p. 82: Photo courtesy of Heat-N-Glo.

Index

Complete Guide to Bathrooms
Complete Guide to Ceramic & Stone Tile
Complete Guide to Creative Landscapes
Complete Guide to Decks
Complete Guide to Easy Woodworking Projects
Complete Guide to Flooring
Complete Guide to Home Carpentry
Complete Guide to Home Masonry
Complete Guide to Home Plumbing
Complete Guide to Home Wiring
Complete Guide to Kitchens
Complete Guide to Landscape Construction
Complete Guide to Outdoor Wood Projects
Complete Guide to Painting & Decorating
Complete Guide to Roofing & Siding
Complete Guide to Trim & Finish Carpentry
Complete Guide to Windows & Doors
Complete Guide to Wood Storage Projects
Complete Guide to Yard & Garden Features
Complete Outdoor Builder
Complete Photo Guide to Home Repair
Complete Photo Guide to Home Improvement

ISBN 1-58923-248-8

ISBN 1-58923-092-2

ISBN 1-58923-094-9

CREATIVE PUBLISHING INTERNATIONAL

18705 LAKE DRIVE EAST
CHANHASSEN, MN 55317

WWW.CREATIVEPUB.COM